THE BARE THING

Lukowski

ISBN: 978-1-915079-21-3

Cover designed by Aaron Kent

Edited and typeset by Aaron Kent

Broken Sleep Books Ltd
Rhydwen,
Talgarreg,
SA44 4HB
Wales

Contents

The Bare Thing

Len Lukowski

Walking To His House

It's not you, it's the blood in you
that flows to the estuaries
where joy and shame meet.

It's not your carefully curated life,
not the version of you
in the stories you tell
about yourself —
meeting friends, working,
phoning home, holidays,
it's an ache

That cuts through
the plans you made,
a need to be filled
that bypasses
the frontal lobe,
screams *now*,
this is the body I have, this is yours,
ours, until the silent walk
across the graveyard
and back home.

Fox cull

In the bins of London are foxes,
hundreds of them, healthy and well-fed
on junk food.
Stalking through gardens
mauling babies
congregating together and attacking old women,
ripping the throats out of Vicars and Priests,
bombing the Houses of Parliament
and setting fire to the House of Lords.
Eating charity workers,
breaking into Buckingham Palace
setting up a guillotine
and beheading the royal family.
Climbing up Big Ben
and detonating themselves one by one,
sleek furry limbs flying everywhere
until all of London is on fire.

Julia Roberts

I was in bed with Julia Roberts, drinking wine at her Hollywood mansion in Notting Hill. She wore the slinkiest of garments and kept touching me. When I leaned in to kiss her, she froze for a couple of seconds then moved away, kept talking as though nothing had happened.

Soon she stood up, began putting on her dress and saying we had to go. We had to get ready or we'd be late for the party her Hollywood friends were having. Now it was my turn to freeze. She had not consented to that kiss. Was I another one of those creepy Hollywood men? Was I Harvey Weinstein?

'Are you ok? Are you coming?' she asked.

I said, 'Are we were alright?' Told her I was sorry for trying to kiss her if it's not what she wanted.

'Hey, it's OK. It's just I've never been with a woman before.'

'I'm not a woman.'

'You know what I mean.' I did. 'I love hanging out with you though, it's so boring spending all my time with those posh, rich people, you're much more fun.' I nodded.

After the party we lay in bed together in our underwear, drunk on expensive wine. Julia Roberts kept touching my arm and thigh but every time I moved towards her, she retreated, turning away from me to the glue and scissors and craft book laid out on the desk beside her bed. Easter crafts, she explained, and began cutting, but soon the cycle would begin again. She would touch me then retreat. After a while I gave up, lay back, and stared at the ceiling, eyes focussed on the tiniest speck of dirt her cleaner had missed. And I kept staring, even as Julia Roberts got up and silently left the room.

Hopeful Monster

1.

A hopeful monster follows me,
begging as only good boys can,
fur curls and moves
like the sky in a Van Gogh painting.

It tries to dig beneath
the front door
arranges itself
upon the stairs
belly to carpeted step
snout through railing
right legs tucked, left legs hanging,
does not deviate from eye contact
and neither do I.

I don't know what it is
anymore to want something as much
as it does watching me eat.
Outsource my longing
to this small beast,
fur like blue flames,
in the hope that one day
we can become each other.

2.

I watch the man come home I want
to climb inside his body,
freakishly pink as a Sphynx cat
aside from errant hairs
around his snout
and crown
and that second skin
he's always wearing.

Sometimes I pity him,
his body's become strange to me,
still I want it back.
I miss the days when I could reach stuff.

Lately the man's been acting strange,
opening tin after tin of my food,
pressing his face inside and
finishing the contents with one inhale.
He doesn't need me anymore,
all I ever do is watch.

Smiling Devil

Hey
Not much.
Relaxing
How about?
Hard?
Yeah
Me too
Hot

Wish it was
All over
Running
So you can feel
Daddy
I am you
With your
Against me
Shoot

Missed you
Not close
Drain those
Empty
I didn't think
It's just
Maybe
It's just
It's just I get so stuck
I get so stuck all the way down there

Alone with your sleeping body

I could not rest, even after fucking,
jaw clenched, shoulders locked,
us tangled up in sticky heat.

How do you sleep like this?
Curtainless window open to the traffic
outside, lights on, bedroom door open
letting in the constant hum
of your fridge.

I think about leaving. Back home,
alone, a cooler, easier place,
environment under my control.
Instead, I sink into your spine
and stop resisting
the relentless noise and heat
—your fridge and the cars
form an orchestra—
organs growing heavy,
muscles turning limp.

A green ballet dancer
hangs by its feet
from your window,
the universe is
closing now, only
white noise remains

Need

necesito ache drool slobber spit on knees begging step through the screen to touch the things inside want reach in stretch out ich brauche multiple tabs open at the same time going round in circles greedy child greedy fuckpig j'ai besoin forgive me i'm always wanting something to rub up against and warm myself a gaping hole pleading to be filled wanting to be lost inside ich liebe ich liebe dich sorry for being here please crave open wound/your legs begging to be filled so desperate you can't be real dream of collapsing forwards inflatable cushion of air to take your weight message sent when drunk never answered those expectant eyes brutally longing wanting to reach in and reclaim the things you lost

Ceiling

The briefs
with the harness
lie on the floor
as new
dry unused.
The dick rests
at the bottom
of the bag
attracting
tiny flecks
of dirt
to its
surface
7 inches
permanently erect
permanently useless.
And all I can think of
is lying next to you sleeping,
junk swollen up like
some monster
out of Borges nose
stinging,
coming down
and staring up
at the ceiling.

Cock

Cock-blocked, I told her
But how would you even— ?
That's the trouble with straight people
no imagination.

If I'd said the actual words
'Home? With me? Now?' instead
of just implied it
if I hadn't told her so much
about myself
or expanded on what I did say —
I swear they're just like muscles
slightly bigger
slightly different shape —
if I'd been more like those guys,
spoke less,
if she didn't know
if I wasn't

Anal

I want to bend over and take it like a man

                A hole where my pleasure centre should be

      Entered pleasurably only once, twice maybe

I know pain is part of the joy but always the tension, the hanging on

The client I told I wouldn't, maybe a finger or two, who said ok
and forced his whole fist in
and I didn't say stop exactly I said we'd have to stop *soon*
so it wasn't exactly   not that the police would
he had orange skin and played Vivaldi

The lover who liked to see me cry during sex
obsessed with entering   though we always had to end before we got going
she told me she enjoyed that brief
look of pain   exquisite moment of violation
as the silicon entered   I said I liked it too

That one Grindr guy was a revelation when we'd fucked enough
the other way   I opened and was hungry for it.
        I remember the dark fur of his chest against my back,
            how the weight of him made me relax.

The rubber-clad skinhead guy in the club
                who fucked me raw   I'd never even heard of PrEP
      kept asking him to come in me
truly a thrill
               that drive towards

A hole that holds the body together

One time my therapist suggested I get to know my arse
        so I smeared a butt plug with lube   amazed at the ease
with which the thing slipped   inside me
that night I dreamt of *Hollyoaks*, the episode where Luke gets raped,
in the dream it was Toby

XY

I saw X last night and much as I want to get on with them and be friends, I fucking hate them. I dreamt a dream and X was in it and the sight of X filled me with such sadness it was physically painful, as though my heart was literally breaking. It soon became too much and I had to wake up. I guess it was the sadness I'd never be with Y in any kind of committed way because X wouldn't allow it. And whatever, I guess Y doesn't want that anyway. When I woke up, the sadness had gone, replaced by anger. I shut my eyes again and there were zombies coming for me, though they moved slowly, my feet were paralysed and my terror was immense as they closed ranks. Finally there was nothing, save the massive desire for cock. Sucking dick for tokens to rides at the fairground at Coney Island on a bleak and windy day.

Table

The calmest I ever felt
I was sedated
upon the
surgeon's table

Vein embracing drip
morphine pumping out
morphine pumping in.

Those are the conditions
under which you can
really let go

finally let them enter
like crying
in front of your father.

What could be more intimate
than a body breathing
without shame

shutting off each
nervous section
of the brain

being cut open
letting someone
open you

A Good Life

And how do you tell your parents
who worked so hard that you might lead a good life
that you don't want to lead a good life?
That all you want to do
is go outside and stick your nose
in wet dirt like a mole.

Leave this sterile place
that is lit like a hospital ward,
go out into the streets of autumn,
sunny and cold, spend everything you have
in empty Chelsea pubs,
belly up on the bar as
whiskey warms your insides.

When night comes
wade into the freezing water
beneath the bridge,
dirty and pure.

At 4am shiver
beneath a blanket as
kind people bring you cups of tea and smile,
asking things your parents never could.
They are your parents now, and you are
leading a good life. All you have to do is breathe.

Ask Me About My Abortion

'Are you a doctor?' Heckled at the entrance. Rain beats down. 'Against God's plan!' I want to tell them —the women doped up on Jesus, the men in raincoats dripping like wet puppies— friends, you don't know the half of it.

I'll tell you what, that didn't happen, like these cramps in my stomach aren't happening now, *ow fuck. Ow!* Ask me about my abortion. I wear the badge, get told I'm a sick fuck.

A chorus of 'Shame!' penetrates the waiting room. I thought the women sat here would stare but they're too lost in their own trauma. To my surprise the receptionist just nods as though I am nothing unusual, she's been briefed. So thankful for that crumb.

I pass through the exit clutching my stomach to shouts of, 'Murderer!' Get in the taxi, lean my head against the window. It takes a second for the driver to chastise me for touching the glass. 'You'll make it dirty'.

Outside the clinic they're singing, 'Life is a precious gift' but all I feel is shame my body could let me down so badly.

Before

One morning, still drunk and cranked up on caffeine, basking in a post-fuck glow, you will proudly text your friend declaring you've just had sex with a guy off Grindr. Some guy who's never had sex with anyone with a vagina. You will feel like you've achieved. You are a pioneer in a land of dick pics and hairy torsos. You're not like other men, but you're still a man, and your ability to pick up on the gayest of apps proves it.

In the afternoon the hangover will set in and you will ask yourself if the events of last night were really that great. You will recall the anxious questions you asked him, seeking to pre-empt any disappointment your body may provide: 'Do I look how you expected me to look? Did you think I'd be more masculine? Have you ever had sex like that before? We don't have to fuck like that.' You will recall how, when he first took your binder off, you looked down at your chest, embarrassed. How, lying naked, skin on skin, you couldn't help but feel your body as feminised next to his, how the thought kept running through your head, *but he likes men, what does he want with* me? How, between fucks, on his bed, swigging cheap white wine, he asked what your name was *before*, and probably this was just natural human curiosity, but what if you were unconvincing as a man? How he'd asked what kind of girl you'd been, if you ever had long hair, if he could see a picture of you 'as a woman'. You got out your phone and showed him a picture of yourself taken at a drag night you'd gone to, dressed as a garish queen, 'Victoria Peckham'. He didn't see the funny side. 'No. I meant *before*.' When he at last sensed your discomfort, he assured you he didn't have a fetish. But it's not like you were there for his personality. Maybe he was your fetish.

Once the hangover lifts you will shrug off all the awkward stuff with Smiths' lyrics: *'Why ponder life's complexities when the leather runs smooth on the passenger seat?'* But you will know that, even before the stupid drunken lack of protection, before the horrified looks on the faces of the pharmacists at your attempt to explain why someone who looks like you needs the morning after pill, before the lonely trek to the sexual health clinic, where the nurse has to call another nurse who phones a hostile-seeming doctor to work out what to do with you, before the course of PEP, before any of that, complexities already get in the way.

That night, you will go to bed, thinking of the way his cum hit your stomach in the early hours, wrapped in the arms of your girlfriend, who just wouldn't understand.

t

there has been no shortage of polls

Malignant aversion has recently had an extraordinary opportunity

to demonstrate its power

treated like an unprecedented sexual threat

a crisis over the entire framing of knowledge about the human body

At the highest levels   there have been criminal delays in

treatment, the obsession with

more to do with   fears than a concern for

used as a pretext to 'justify' calls for increasing legislation   of

Try keeping up   through   press, and you'll remain   ignorant.

TV treats us to nauseating processions of yuppie women announcing   to the
world that

scaring them   costing them a fucking fortune, for our "lifestyle"

Almost all media coverage has been aimed at   as if

were not part of the audience

representation is very different from reflection

of what it means to be

bodies that we carry within us

it is perhaps necessary to accept the pain of embracing

Testosterone 1

I thought I'd just try it out.

I didn't think it would be a big deal.

I didn't know it would be so connected to my sense of self.

I didn't know I had a sense of self.

I lay in bed like a stone wondering what I was doing.

Testosterone 2
After Rilke

Once you have inhabited it from every angle
you cannot unknow the absurdity
of classifying the body with a hasty

glance towards the face or groin.
Shatter the borders of who you are,
it's always changing — hesitant

specimen of manhood
never predicted
never foresaw
how the meanings
would shift

from the lab
to the needle
to the butt cheek
to the vein
to the heart
to your bed,
a cat, jumping
out of one box
and into another.

You must keep
changing your life.
Even after death
your body will
continue to
revise itself.

Testosterone 3

You will seek another dopamine hit everywhere you go, never satisfied. You will be so insecure about your masculinity you will buy Bulldog grooming products and Mansize tissues but you cannot give up nail varnish. You will marvel at the size of your cock on hormones, Robert Mapplethorpe's models got nothing on your whole one inch. You will agonise over what to wear on a date with a straight girl as if clothes are your biggest problem not your short stature, your dicklessness. You will withhold the truth sometimes because you know whole perceptions can change once a body is envisaged naked with different parts or maybe you're just self-obsessed, you will get more self-obsessed. You will start to sound like the guys you hated before testosterone, guys who had to announce to YouTube every time they grew an extra chin hair, you will resist announcing 80% of the time but you'll really really want to, you won't get a YouTube channel because you're too old. You will become sick of people thinking you're 14 when you're 35 will grow a beard but the beard will be a smattering of hairs the kind a 14 year old trying to look like an adult might grow and one day, when you're on holiday in some place very different to your regular life, the wind will mercilessly howl through the valleys like the gothic novels said it would and you will contemplate your body as warm water hits it from the shower, a landscape of fur and skin and scars and ambivalence and you will feel like it's really yours. You will feel ambivalence slipping away year after year much to the horror of your former self. You will grow hungrier, hornier, grumpier, heavier, sometimes feel stupider, and will come to take pleasure in all those things and in the heights and depths of puberty, missing only the ability to cry.

Head

And in the heat
you become animal
part animal
part dog
you're panting
in the blurry air
show me your teeth

the day so hot
goes on forever
our bodies
hit the scummy surface
of the water and
into the slimy darkness
of the bottom
we emerge
to become each other

animals fighting
sniffing
mounting
rutting
collapsing
at least in my head

The Resonance

One night plunging into
the darkness of my room
I took every word
I'd ever used for you
and every bad thing
you'd read of me
and planted them
like flowers
inside my brain
till morning.

And in the gloom of the valley
at the edge of town
where the snow fell
I made a video,
played it back, the
sound of white static
on silent flurry and you
stood there behind me
a voice in the ripples of the stream
vibrations in the water
shaking trees
quietly forming the words
nothing can grow
in the shadow of history.

When you were gone,
safe from language,

I listened harder
to the muteness of the snow,
the water in the valley
flowing beneath my room,
and the waves of static,
flattening themselves
and then repeating.

Room World

The world becomes your flat and your flat becomes your room.

Your room gets smaller.

Objects closing in —
   clotheshorse, rucksack, plastic bag, bike.

Propped against the walls, piles of books form the edge of everything.

In the morning the birds outside
      seem louder, as if this is a particularly
      joyous moment in history.

Ghost trains pass your window, full of empty seats.
      Ghost planes overhead, no one makes plans,
         no one fucks strangers.

The closer the edges get, the more you feel embraced
      never needing to put up a hand
         or explain

to live and die amongst your things
nest between the pillows
of your tiny planet
leave the universe to the birds

The Virus

The thing about the virus is
The virus can only live on
The virus can live for at least   outside the body
The virus will be around for   but not until
The virus will be gone by
The virus comes from   and   but definitely not
The virus won't be as bad as   of the year   but worse than   of the year
The virus has mutated into   but will not become
To avoid the virus you must   but under no circumstances should you
If you have the virus it is imperative that you   for at least
You won't know you have the virus until   maybe not ever
                                                No one knows anything about the virus

Acts of Love

No one is entitled to love

least of all me

to be loved

is to excuse the hate we're forged in

I have always known this

love is creepy and claustrophobic

needy and narcissistic

mouth to mouth

when all the air is toxic

bodies are disappointing

sex is better in your head

How can you love me and not be angry

I was born with so much joy already in me

that got subtracted

in the dance between what's joyous and

what's forbidden

Songs of love echo underclass betrayal

touch the bare thing

lick my legs, I'm on fire

relent and love

in a darkened room

I'm not just talking sexually

I mean

mouth to

36

about the things they say in the papers?

The things I care for most are the parts you cannot love

foreign objects

it doesn't count unless there are stakes

don't fall in love while the building blazes

don't fall in love while the camps fill up around you

and pretend it matters

like a Stepford Wife.

What's the point in a love

that doesn't come in the form of an act

that would wrench at

the hand that is choking the neck of us all?

That doesn't help the ones they've come for?

my scarred chest

cavern beneath the ribs

red blood cells

it doesn't count if there's no risk

bleed

I know

you can do that

I know I'm just the same

relent and love

the one thing about

me

that always made you

turn away

London

I give full submission in company. Walk through the city at night thinking how empty it got without you. When I'm alone I'll mine my heart for anything that's left and the red of the blood reminds me how happy I am.

We were lost, you can't say we weren't you and your self-righteous rightness, me and my extreme insecurity, always trying to please, never knowing. Full submission in company, you give it as well: your personality has been subsumed into hers and I can't find a home in you anymore.

Every night I dreamt of strolling to my death while you danced to the Pet Shop Boys. You were having a baby because you knew you wouldn't be around forever and you wanted it not to have been for nothing, but I don't want a baby, so what the hell do I do? And your sister she was there as well, she'd accused me of the most terrible crime I'm pretty sure I didn't commit, but at night still she and I would meet on the Heath and fuck so tenderly by the water as though nothing were amiss. In the morning it dawned on me the charges still stood and my heart beat fast in terror.

Every time I see you I have to drink a bottle of whiskey. Half a bottle in, Googling 'sort my life out'. If you were erased from my consciousness it would be no bad thing.

I search the whole of the Internet for the right kind of music — some sound to make me feel OK.

I'm sorry for what happened.

Outside now, outside is safe. Don't go.

Your Haunt

Some time in your thirties you'll realise
you've become a ghost that haunts the city
and all the friends you came here with
have moved on.
It's been so long since you were
touched, even by the fur of a dog,
you're not sure you have a body anymore.

Snow in the cemetery silences your
foot steps, couples passing, parents
with their kids sledging — a movie
with the sound on mute.
Only know you can be seen
when the sky starts to darken
and a stranger turns to you, says,
that way's locked, you can't go there,
and without thinking you obey,

turn and stumble back to where you came from.

Notes & Acknowledgements

Fox Cull: In 2013 there was extensive press coverage of a fox attacking a human baby in a London garden. Sections of the UK media responded to the attack by calling for mass fox culls both in London and nationally, as did the Mayor of London at that time, Boris Johnson, who suggested fox hunting be introduced in the city.

Hopeful Monster: draws its title from a book of short stories and single story by Hiromi Goto, Hopeful Monsters

t: is an erasure of 'Is The Rectum A Grave' by Leo Bersani, the line 'representation is very different from reflection' draws on ideas by Stuart Hall

Testosterone 1 - 3: Testosterone affects everyone differently. Nothing described in these poems should be taken as the definitive transmasculine truth.

Testosterone 2: is a rewriting of Archaic Torso of Apollo by Rainer Maria Rilke

Acts of Love: contains lyrics by the Manic Street Preachers and PJ Harvey

'Fox Cull' previously published in *The Ofi Press*, 'Ceiling' previously published in *York:Mix*, 'Cock' previously published in *LossLit*, 'Before' previously published in *Grinding Poetry*, 'The Virus', 'London' and a version of 'Julia Roberts' previously published in *MIR Online*, 'Your Haunt' previously published in the *Live Canon 2018 Anthology*, 'Hopeful Monster' and a version of 'Alone with your Sleeping Body' previously published in *Anthropocene Poetry*.

Grateful to the following people for your support and encouragement in poetry and/or life whilst these poems were coming into being: Swithun Cooper, Robin Duval, Martina Evans, Bob Henderson, Madeleine Hunter, Nazmia Jamal, Sarah Keenan, Aaron Kent, Andrew McMillan, Humaira Saeed, Melissa Rakshana Steiner, Sal Tomcat, Lindsay Tudor-Kasbohm, Faryal Velmi and everyone I have inevitably forgotten.

LAY OUT YOUR UNREST

Lightning Source UK Ltd.
Milton Keynes UK
UKHW011132161122
412293UK00002B/30